40 Meditations for Renewing Hope

ALWAYS FOUND

Finding God In Perpetual Advent

DR. SHAUNTA D. SCROGGINS

Extreme Overflow Publishing
Dacula, GA
USA

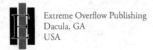

Extreme Overflow Publishing
Dacula, GA
USA

Extreme Overflow Publishing

A Brand of Extreme Overflow Enterprises, Inc

P.O. Box 1811

Dacula, GA 30019

www.extremeoverflow.com

Send feedback to info@extremeoverflow.com

Printed in the United States of America

Library of Congress Catalogin-Publication

Data is available for this title. ISBN: 978-1-7379262-1-4

40 Meditations for Renewing Hope

ALWAYS FOUND

Finding God in Perpetual Advent

DR. SHAUNTA D. SCROGGINS

To those who feel lost,

and when lost,

look for God.

We are never lost,

but always found –

in God's love, promises, and abounding grace.

Contents

Preface

Introduction

ADVENT

Contents (cont'd)

PREFACE

On a December evening during my first public Bible teaching opportunity, I used Advent and Incarnation among other seasonally appropriate words. It was nearly 20 years ago. I loved the traditional holiday season then, and I still love this time of year.

For one, people are generally nicer. Society move from the dog-eat-dog and human-kill-human mindset to a verbalized peace and goodwill hope. Two, there's an inundation of positive messages like at no other time of year — give, serve, help, remember, love, peace, soldiers, etc. We settle in for Christmas movies, prep for traditions, and soften the hardened layers we thought needed in the earlier parts of the year. Three, we embrace the awareness of our blessings. We review the year and realize the hard parts did not define our year but defined our character.

I look forward to the Advent season because *hope finds me and connects with my wavering faith.* I know that during the Advent, according to the scriptures, that *I can expect to see the Christ child manifest in my life.* Prophetic promises yield a King in a manger, and *I can rightfully look for a tangible expression of Advent.*

Advent is the time we take our cues from the story of the birth of Jesus. <u>We become like shepherds</u> and consider our journey to meet Him. <u>We look to the east</u> for the guiding star. We start to look for Jesus' birth in our lives in "manger" places, places that inspire us to <u>make room in our INNer selves</u> for His love, light, and lessons. <u>We even become better observers, like the stable animals,</u> and protect our environments better with the love of God.

Advent is Power

Christmas comes with history, traditions, lovers, haters, and a demeanor of its own. People of faith and people who claim no faith either look to or run from Christmas due to triggers of memory, celebration, or loss and grief. In our family plans, or our escape plans, we can miss the fact that the carols and nativity sets help us imagine a baby born to save the world. Advent is God's transcendent reach for humanity, and an invitation to see how his life can impact our lives. Advent is neutral to the arguments of when Jesus was born, Christmas being a pagan holiday, and the problems of commercialism because advent is fact. Jesus was born and his birth or advent crossed through many lives to offer us broad perspective and significance on encountering Him today.

The word advent means an appearance; and contained in the advent story is one reminder after another that we are found, loved, seen, and heard, even with our fears and questions. Nod at Santa, bells, and ornaments if you want. Enjoy the decorations and traditions. But during Advent, look for Jesus. Look to watch Him born in the neglected areas of your life. Look for His entrance into the storage of our souls.

Advent Never Disappoints

In the manger, we find Jesus. In the manger, we bow before Him, and our lives crown Him King again. What do bowing and crowning Jesus look like? It is the acts of yielding and surrender. As we realize the greatness of his love, of how far it can expand around our lives and experiences, we yield ourselves over and over. Bowing in our hearts, thoughts, and actions is our willingness to submit. Crowning him king is our acknowledgement of his lordship in our lives, and our promise to follow and obey him.

The beautiful truth of Advent today is that if we cultivate childlike faith, we can live in expectation all year long. Twenty years after teaching my first Bible study in the Advent season, and I still have courageous faith for the presence of God to appear in every place. I call the Advent "wild card season" because I believe that anything can happen. It's like the idea of "Christmas miracles" but so much more. I want everyone to have this kind of hope during the holidays and realize the marvelous love of God in the Advent. Feeling lost can happen gradually or suddenly, and I offer these 40 meditation readings to remind us that we can have hope in the presence of God coming in as many different ways as Jesus' birth came to the people involved in the story. These meditation reminders are not dated, so you can spend as much time as you need on any entry, pondering on the Lord's ability to reach you where you are. Read daily, weekly, and all year, not just during the holidays.

INTRODUCTION

My pastor reminded me through a sermon how God will use the foolish things to confound the wise and bring about His purpose. He talked about "crazy stuff" that will happen, and that locked within it is a blessing or reward for us.

Today, we can remember Mary the mother of Jesus in this way. She was an engaged young girl pregnant by the Holy Ghost. I mean, how did she even try to explain that? We honor her today… but truthfully, we rejoice for only one immaculate conception (the saints today differ little from the saints of old).

Once she knew for sure God was working through her, she endured — social pressure, emotional pressure, the risk of Joseph leaving, even "crazy" birthing conditions. In the end, though, the Lord arrived.

In all the "extra crazy" that happens this time of year, I want to remind us of THE ADVENT. This is the time of year that THE LORD ARRIVES. This is the big point of this devotional because he was born for us all. The Advent is the greatest story on earth, one where we can come to realize that we were never lost, but always found. Step aside from the technical soap boxes about the trees and decorations, the pagan holiday discussion, Jesus' real birthday, the lie of Santa and so on. Consider the point coming across amid the crazy stuff — **HE IS HERE.** Jesus being present reminds us of the potential in an encounter with him. His arrival means that the way we see everything can change.

The longer we live, I think the better we understand how cycles of vulnerability and lostness can happen. Questions go unanswered. Circumstances without reason leave us without good resolve. Whether gradually or suddenly, there are times that we feel lost and unable to reconnect in ways that are life giving and beneficial. Our feelings speak as loud as our needs, sometimes. I want us to know that we are found in Christ, so we can make Advent announcements to our feelings like the angels did to Mary and Joseph. Announcements like:

God loves me.

I have the help of heaven.

God sees me.

God has a wonderful plan for my life, that includes others.

My dreams give me wise, godly instruction.

God protects me.

God is for me.

My faith has a legacy.

I may feel lost, but I am really found. God knows exactly where I am.

As you turn the pages of this devotional and confront any lostness or lack of connection with the powerful truths of Advent, remember that you are on the receiving end of revelation. Let the wonder and beauty of God coming to earth for you encourage your heart and elevate your mindset. *See where you are as the beginning of beautiful.* Lean into this part of your process. Make notes on the page and add your details to the devotional. Do not rush the healing that will come to your mind and heart as you embrace the Advent. We have come to a part of the process worth savoring and enjoying. The Lord is indeed kind to us and wants to minister to us. Selah, and with lots of love!

He hath made everything beautiful in its time: also he hath set the world in their heart, so that no man can find out the work that God maketh from the beginning to the end. Ecclesiastes 3:11

ADVENT

01

Finding God When There's A Threat

¹ Now after Jesus was born in Bethlehem of Judea in the days of Herod the king, behold, wise men from the east came to Jerusalem, ² saying, "Where is he who has been born king of the Jews? For we saw his star when it rose and have come to worship him."

Matthew 2:1-2 ESV

The Days of Herod

This phrase signifies the reign of Herod. What kind of man was King Herod? What kinds of things happened under his reign? Here's a short list:

- Ruthlessness, killing his wife and legal heirs to the throne

- Large and successful builder of great buildings, including a Jewish temple

- Skilled negotiator and diplomat

- Jealous of competition, namely Jesus as the King of the Jews

- Had all the male infants in Bethlehem killed

  hoping to kill Jesus

Despite Herod's worst deeds, he could not prevent the birth of Jesus. Today, bad bosses, toxic leaders, evil plots . . . none of them can stop the presence of God appearing in our lives. This is an advent truth to recall all year long: nothing and no one can stop the presence of God from showing up.

What or who seems like a hindrance to you? Tim Sheets, author of Planting the Heavens, said, "The mountain is as big as it's going to get, but you're still growing." Even if the obstacle is as terrifying a presence as Herod the Great, it is still what it is. You, though, are growing in grace and in your knowledge of

God (2 Pet. 3:18), as well as in perspective about the obstacle. Your ability to conquer the threat is bigger than the threat. Remember that. The presence of God brings assurance that you have help to address threatening circumstances.

Father, I acknowledge that you are bigger and greater than any Herod-like presence. I agree that nothing and no one can stop your presence in my life. I pray this in Jesus' name. AMEN.

02

Finding God In Unbelief

[18] And Zechariah said to the angel, "How shall I know this? For I am an old man, and my wife is advanced in years." [19] And the angel answered him, "I am Gabriel. I stand in the presence of God, and I was sent to speak to you and to bring you this good news. [20] And behold, you will be silent and unable to speak until the day that these things take place, because you did not believe my words, which will be fulfilled in their time."

Luke 1:18-20 ESV

Sometimes, We Don't Believe We Will Receive Our Heart's Desire.

Either that, or we are completely astonished at the arrival of divine timing. Sometimes, waiting for our heart's desire makes our hearts sick (See Proverbs 13:12). Zechariah and Elizabeth waited for so long, that even in the presence of a true angelic visitation, Zechariah could not wrap his mind around he and his wife Elizabeth having a child.

After years of waiting, hoping, and maybe wavering, the time finally comes. We each get an "and it came to pass" eventually, for some prayer requests. What happens to waning hope, though? It makes for a tender and sometimes hurting heart and can lead to unbelief. Sometimes, like Zechariah, we are struck dumb or unable to speak because of unbelief. And we are left to watch the scenes play out in our lives.

Ask yourself, "Am I prepared for the Lord to visit me and declare that the time is now?" Advent is the time we renew our hope in Immanuel, God with us. We reaffirm our confidence in His omnipresence and His manifestation because he causes us to believe again. He is here, and He is coming to help our unbelief.

Father, I speak to the cast down and weary parts of my soul. Hope in God! Thank you for remembering my petition and thank you for answering. I pray this in Jesus' name. AMEN.

03

Finding God Where
There Are No Vacancies

And she gave birth to her firstborn son and wrapped him in swaddling cloths and laid him in a manger, because there was no place for them in the inn.

Luke 2:7 ESV

Sometimes, There Is Just Not Enough Room.

"Making do" is a popular phrase in the Southern United States and means to adjust or to be content with a temporary solution. This is one of the greatest parts of the Advent season. God understands "making do," and Mary and Joseph experience it.

There are two considerations for the text saying that "there was no place for them in the inn." One thought is that if Joseph and Mary looked for lodging in public accommodations, the options would have been shelters for people and animals. The other thought is that if Joseph and Mary stayed with relatives, then there were no more guest rooms to house them. Bethlehem was a small place, and with everyone traveling home for the census, it is likely that all the rooms were unavailable.

Making do is a thing we all must do at some point. We have a plan and try to work it, and when we arrive, we must pivot because there is no room. Adjustment, though, is not a bad thing. Advent is a reminder that greatness can be born through adjustment. Let us not be distracted by the circumstances or the pushing out in spaces that seem fully occupied. God has a way of creating space for us and allowing us to birth his marvelous purpose.

Father, thank you for my valuable life. Help me to remember that tight places and occupied spaces are no match for the divine purpose in me. There will be room to be and do as you have called me. I pray this in Jesus' name. AMEN.

04

Finding God While Wondering

[18] The disciples of John reported all these things to him. And John, [19] calling two of his disciples to him, sent them to the Lord, saying, "Are you the one who is to come, or shall we look for another?"

Luke 7:18-19 ESV

We Can Love Jesus With All Our Hearts, And Still Wonder . . .

John the Baptist, cousin to Jesus, had a ministry calling to prepare the way for Jesus. He served, warned, confronted, and even baptized Jesus. At the time of Jesus' ministry, John was in prison and would be killed. John was faithful to the calling and yet, at the exciting time of the revelation of who Jesus was, John wanted to be sure. John wondered.

Jesus, are you the one who is to come, or should we look for another?

It is possible to miss some obvious signs that Jesus is present. The spirit of advent organically births fresh hope and anticipation for the revelation of Jesus Christ. This hope and expectation are not limited to the winter months or holidays. Think bigger. Advent is the announcement of an entrance, of one coming. From now on, let's speak to our hearts and declare that we have found the One for whom we searched.

Father, thank you for revealing yourself to me when I wonder if you are coming to address a need in my life. I am grateful that you allow me to wonder, and comfort me with your report of miracles. I am looking for no other. I pray this in Jesus' name. AMEN.

05

Finding God in a Long Wait

But they had no child, because Elizabeth was barren, and both were advanced in years.

Luke 1:7 ESV

Have You Ever Waited A Long Time For God To Make Good On A Promise?

Elizabeth is amazing! She waited a long time – a very long time – to be pregnant, carry a child, and give birth. The Lord even made sure Elizabeth had a celebration partner in her cousin Mary. Her husband, Zechariah, was struck silent until she gave birth. Imagine having to create a new system of communication! For months, Elizabeth heard her own voice in her home.

What if today is THE day that the long wait is over?

What if this week is THE week that the long wait is over?

What if this month is THE month that the long wait is over?

What if this year is THE year that the long wait is over?

I know, I'm not fond of "follow the carrot" questions either, yet the questions are valid. There is a wise saying that seems appropriate here: God did not bring you this far just to bring you this far. Waiting happens, and in life there must be at least one very long wait. In waiting though, we can find our way to an encounter with God.

If you are in a long wait right now, then allow your mind to relax in the wait. Think about ways to keep looking for and expecting God's presence. Think about the dream again. Read about Elizabeth and let the Holy Spirit inspire hope.

Father, sometimes I get impatient or disheartened when I wait on you. I tend to have in my mind how things should go. I submit to your will and ask you to help me wait on you. Keep my mind in perfect peace, so that I will not focus on the frustrations of waiting. I pray this in Jesus' name. AMEN.

06

Finding God in Tough Decisions

[19] And her husband Joseph, being a just man and unwilling to put her to shame, resolved to divorce her quietly. [20] But as he considered these things, behold, an angel of the Lord appeared to him in a dream, saying, "Joseph, son of David, do not fear to take Mary as your wife, for that which is conceived in her is from the Holy Spirit.

Matthew 1:19-20 ESV

Sometimes, We Just Need God To Settle The Issue.

I cannot imagine being a man (for one!), wanting to marry a woman, and then finding out God called her to be and do what no one else would ever receive a call to be or do after her. God's calling created difficult circumstances, and Joseph was about to bow out and take his exit. He loved Mary, planned to make her his wife, and in the courtship learned she was pregnant by the Holy Ghost.

Joseph had a tough decision to make between the stigma of the culture or God's will. He is an example of how God guides us through supernatural experiences in our everyday life. We have plans, like Joseph's plan to marry Mary. We encounter the unexpected, like Joseph hears the news about an immaculate conception. We wonder what the right thing to do is, and we sometimes want to run away.

Then God shows up and speaks, brings clarity, and offers a path to continue. In Joseph's case, God comforts and endorses the union with Mary. To us too, God will speak and settle the issue.

Father, thank you for showing us how to trust you when we wonder which way is right. Thank you for speaking at the right time, so that we make the right choice. However you speak to us, we welcome your voice. I pray this in Jesus' name. AMEN.

07

Finding God in Sweet Faith

²⁶ In the sixth month the angel Gabriel was sent from God to a city of Galilee named Nazareth, ²⁷ to a virgin betrothed to a man whose name was Joseph, of the house of David. And the virgin's name was Mary. ²⁸ And he came to her and said, "Greetings, O favored one, the Lord is with you!" ³⁸ And Mary said, "Behold, I am the servant of the Lord; let it be to me according to your word."

And the angel departed from her.

Luke 1:26-28, 38 ESV

Are You a Taker?

Occasionally, we have to ask ourselves if we give before we receive, or because we receive. We can sometimes approach God this way – only wanting to receive and hesitant to give.

Young Mary, in the Advent account, shows us what we can give God that he values greatly. Trust. After receiving one of the most challenging calls to ministry ever, Mary trusts. I want to say she simply trusts, but we do not know that agreeing to carry and birth God was simple.

Mary gave God her trust when the angel visited her with the message that she was chosen, along with the details of her assignment. We can struggle mightily with what we see. How can we trust God, like Mary, when we receive a supernatural task?

For Mary's reply to be, "Here am I, the servant of the Lord; let it be with me according to your word," I believe trust had been nurtured in Mary's heart. Somehow, Mary learned devotion to God and maintained faith to the degree that when given the biggest charge of her life, her response was availability. No pleading for confirmation or details. No doubts or wavering that we know about. Just, "I am your servant, Lord."

Let us approach each day committing our cares to the Father. Let us see God's errands as a sweet invitation to trust. As with Mary, the Lord will be with us.

Father, I come before you with what you asked me to do. You gave me an assignment, and I:

- *Said yes and want to recommit with trust.*

- *Doubted, and want to say yes, trusting you.*

- *Said no and have been running, but today I want to say yes and trust you.*

With a sober heart, I offer any fears, concerns, questions, and anxiety. I choose you, the God of my gift, and with your help, I will serve you. I pray this in Jesus' name. AMEN.

08

Finding God in the Promised Place

⁴ And Joseph also went up from Galilee, from the town of Nazareth to Judea, to the city of David, which is called Bethlehem, because he was of the house and lineage of David, ⁵ to be registered with Mary, his betrothed, who was with child. ⁶ And while they were there, the time came for her to give birth.

Luke 2:4-6 ESV

Sometimes, We Find God in the Design.

Have you ever made a move or taken a trip for one reason, only to discover that God had other plans? Once past the agitation or wondering, did you realize that God ordered your steps to this place? Mary and Joseph were in Nazareth; that is where we meet them (Lk. 1:26). One command from the emperor required the whole word to return to their hometowns (2:1,3). This is how Mary and Joseph were positioned in Bethlehem.

Advent is a time of presence. In all the movement, we can get caught up and either miss or be late to recognize the Father's involvement. Some believe that God does not care about the details of our carnal existence. In concept, that may be true. But inasmuch as the details are used for God's divine purpose concerning us, Advent proves that God cares about the details that position us in his design. So, if that means for us sending a friend, a trip to the store, or to a beautiful getaway, a car, clothes, or a home, then so be it.

Let us learn to be more flexible in our living. Let us nurture a first response that says, "This could be God," and as a result, cultivate a good attitude toward change. God's design may full well change our plans.

Father, I am willing to end up in Bethlehem. Help me to transition well when the call to move comes. Govern my speech, so that I am filled with more faith and wonder than stalling and complaint. Restore in me the awe of your will being done in my life. I pray this in Jesus' name. AMEN.

09

Finding God in Divine Visitation

[20] But as he considered these things, behold, an angel of the Lord appeared to him in a dream, saying, "Joseph, son of David, do not fear to take Mary as your wife, for that which is conceived in her is from the Holy Spirit . . . [13] Now when they had departed, behold, an angel of the Lord appeared to Joseph in a dream and said, "Rise, take the child and his mother, and flee to Egypt, and remain there until I tell you, for Herod is about to search for the child, to destroy him." . . . [19] But when Herod died, behold, an angel of the Lord appeared in a dream to Joseph in Egypt,

Matthew 1:20, 2:13, 19 ESV

One of the most wonderful feelings is to know that God is with us.

To follow a path believing it to be the right one, and then receive special confirmation, builds our confidence, and affirms our ear to hear our Father. God can, of course, choose to confirm our path or not; when he confirms though, he chooses as well how he will reach us.

Joseph was guided through a process of decision making that included angels. There was a first message of comfort: do not be afraid to marry Mary (Matt. 1:20). Then, after Jesus was born and to be safe from Herod's search to destroy Jesus, an angel warned Joseph to flee to Egypt (2:13). Finally, when Herod died, Joseph received another angelic visitation to announce Jesus' safety and instruct him on where to move his family (2:19).

Advent reminds us that God knows how to reach us with what we need to follow his path. Today, born-again disciples of Jesus have his Holy Spirit living in us. The Holy Spirit will comfort, warn, and guide us on the ordained path. That's good news!

Father, thank you for angelic help. Thank you for all the ways you show your love and care for us through visiting us. For this and more, we are grateful. I pray this in Jesus' name. AMEN.

10

Finding God in Sleep

[20] But as he considered these things, behold, an angel of the Lord appeared to him in a dream, saying, "Joseph, son of David, do not fear to take Mary as your wife, for that which is conceived in her is from the Holy Spirit . . . [13] Now when they had departed, behold, an angel of the Lord appeared to Joseph in a dream and said, "Rise, take the child and his mother, and flee to Egypt, and remain there until I tell you, for Herod is about to search for the child, to destroy him." . . .[19] But when Herod died, behold, an angel of the Lord appeared in a dream to Joseph in Egypt,

Matthew 1:20, 2:13, 19 ESV

Sometimes, God Bypasses Our Waking Minds to Speak While We Sleep.

The Advent account records that God spoke in dreams and gave warnings about how to proceed. The magi received a warning dream to not return to Herod with news of the Christ child. Joseph received three dreams. The angel first appeared to Joseph to calm his fear about marrying a pregnant Mary. He was assured of God's plan. Later, when Herod issued orders to kill baby boys at the ages of two and under, an angel appeared in two dreams to Joseph. Both dreams gave directions; Joseph was to flee to Egypt with his family and then return after Herod died.

Advent reminds us that God has a plan, and we play a part. Also, Advent assures us that God speaks to us when we are afraid and in danger. May we allow the Advent season to open our hearts to the ways of God. And when he speaks, may we be comforted, warned, and instructed for our next steps. Sometimes, we do not know what to do. God can give us a dream, bypass our logic when needed, and grant us peace, safety, and clarity. Let us keep believing.

Father, I make myself available to you, even as I sleep. Grant me dreams with understanding and the interpretation. Cause me to know what you are saying, whether by angel, symbolic, or real-time dreams. My desire is to obey you. I pray this in Jesus' name. AMEN.

11

Finding God in the Preceding Word

They told him, "In Bethlehem of Judea, for so it is written by the prophet"

Matthew 2:5 ESV

Sometimes, We Hear What's Already Been Said.

Advent is a time to remember that present realities are the result of words spoken before. Prophecy is an important part of Jesus' life. One significant act after another, Jesus lives and fulfills prophecy. The details of Jesus' birth were prophesied to give those hundreds of years later a reference point in history, government, theology, and astrology. God spoke broadly then, as he does today.

There are prophecies from the Scriptures, and prophecies through inspired men and women. If we ever come to a place we cannot identify, then I hope we remember to review the prophecies.

Father, thank you for speaking ahead of us into our lives and experiences. Your Word gives us hope. As we navigate this life, please give us vision for the future through the prophetic word. I pray this in Jesus' name. AMEN.

12

Finding God in the Testimony of the Righteous

[25] Now there was a man in Jerusalem, whose name was Simeon, and this man was righteous and devout, waiting for the consolation of Israel, and the Holy Spirit was upon him.

Luke 2:25 ESV

Advent Allows Us the Privilege of Many Points of View.

We see the betrothal of Mary and Joseph, the political threat to Herod, the innkeeper, the decree of Caesar Augustus, and the faithful testimony of Simeon. The Holy Spirit promised Simeon that Simeon would not die until Simeon saw the Messiah.

The reason Simeon got to see the baby Jesus was because of the custom and practice of eighth-day circumcision. Mary and Joseph brought the baby Jesus to Jerusalem to be dedicated to the Lord. Simeon took Jesus, held him, and praised God.

Advent is not new, not since Jesus was born an infant. Advent, observed year to year, extends to us today. Contained in the Advent experience, wisdom, and prophetic utterances over time, is the testimony of the righteous. For many years, faithful men and women learned about a coming Messiah. Simeon got to see Jesus and testify. If we are willing, when we open our eyes in Advent and see; then we, too, will testify.

Father, thank you for the power of your promise, that when fulfilled, gives us a testimony to share. Thank you for the power in our testimonies to share your inspired words with others. Keep giving us the ability to receive and share testimonies. I pray this in Jesus' name. AMEN.

13

Finding God in Covenant

[18] Now the birth of Jesus Christ took place in this way. When his mother Mary had been betrothed to Joseph, before they came together she was found to be with child from the Holy Spirit. [19] And her husband Joseph, being a just man and unwilling to put her to shame, resolved to divorce her quietly. [20] But as he considered these things, behold, an angel of the Lord appeared to him in a dream, saying, "Joseph, son of David, do not fear to take Mary as your wife, for that which is conceived in her is from the Holy Spirit.

Matthew 1:18-20 ESV

Sometimes, We Find God in Covenant.

Joseph wins for most unusual situation with a fiancée. He was betrothed to a pregnant virgin. Betrothed is three things – a noun, an adjective, and a verb. Mary was not a friend or casual acquaintance. Joseph chose Mary for marriage. We do not know how Joseph came to choose Mary, but we may identify with the struggle of creating and establishing lifelong bonds.

(n.) the person to whom one is engaged to be married

(adj.) pledged in marriage

(v.) promised or affianced

Joseph wanted to be Mary's husband, but how would a birth be explained without marring his or Mary's character? He was a righteous man in love, and he decided: I will separate us. Then an angel of the Lord appeared to Joseph and told Joseph not to fear. Mary is telling the truth; this baby is conceived by the Holy Ghost. You can marry her in peace.

I agree with the charge in Mark 10:9 – Therefore what God has joined together, let no one separate. May I add an insight? I am convinced, based on Matthew 1:18-30, that God will help a covenant he creates to stay together. Advent reminds us to pause before making life-altering decisions. God may speak to the unexplainable to keep a covenant together.

Father, highlight for me the covenants in my life and teach me to value them. When circumstances are risky enough for me to walk away, give me your wisdom to know how to act. I pray this in Jesus' name. AMEN.

14

Finding God in Peaceful Waiting

And Mary said, "Behold, I am the servant of the Lord; let it be to me according to your word." And the angel departed from her.

Luke 1:38 ESV

Sometimes, We Have to Make Peace with the Wait.

Of all the wonderful ways to turn the prism on Advent, the waiting is the angle I avoid. I don't like waiting. Of course, whether we like waiting or not does not matter. Waiting is par for the course, and so we must come to terms with waiting. We are in good company, too. Zechariah and Elizabeth, Mary, and Simeon all waited for the manifestation of promise through the Christ child.

Making peace with the wait helps us be less fearful while we wait. Through uncertainty, questions, and the journey to manifestation, there is the wait. Today, let us confront any frustration, impatience, or other feelings about waiting. Let us look the perceived obstacles in the face and throw out the alternate endings. Let us clear our minds, renew our minds in God's Word, declutter our hearts, spend time with Him, and wait.

Father, thank you for the journey. I get to walk with you; and in return, you teach me who you are and reveal who I am. Help me to wait well. I pray this in Jesus' name. AMEN.

15

Finding God in Protection from Danger

[19] But when Herod died, behold, an angel of the Lord appeared in a dream to Joseph in Egypt, [20] saying, "Rise, take the child and his mother and go to the land of Israel, for those who sought the child's life are dead."

Matthew 2:19-20 ESV

Sometimes, There is a Danger That is Unknown to Us.

God's protection is marvelous! He has the foresight to know the actions of others; so do we, but only if he reveals their actions. When we are in danger, when plots are hatching, God knows.

King Herod felt threatened by the announcement of a "King of the Jews" (Matt. 2:3). The wise men journeyed to honor this new king and frightened Herod with the news (vv. 1-2). Chief priests and scribes informed Herod of the prophecies (vv. 5-6). Caught up with the details of the new king and the star, Herod sent the wise men on a mission to find the king and report back (vv. 7-8).

God was greater than Herod and issued three warnings: one to the wise men and two to Joseph, all in dreams by messenger angels. The wise men were warned not to return to Herod (v. 12), which set off Herod's enraged campaign to kill all the children in and around Bethlehem who were two years old and under (v. 16). Before the campaign began, and after Herod's death, Joseph was warned to move to and later depart from Egypt, respectively (vv. 13-14, 19-21).

Father, thank you for being greater than every enemy. Thank you for guiding my life in ways that keep me from unseen dangers. I may not be present when the scheme begins, but you are able to enlighten me and show me how to respond. Thank you for saving my life, again and again. I pray this in Jesus' name. AMEN.

16

Finding God in His Sovereignty

Now the birth of Jesus Christ took place in this way.

Matthew 1:18 ESV

Sometimes, We Wonder What is Going On, and Who Really Has the Answer

I love the word providence. It means the protective care of God. When capitalized as Providence, the word suggests God is understood as the power sustaining and guiding human destiny. The entire advent story – all accounts taken together – owes everything to Providence. The fulfillment of prophecy meant the story had to unfold with some specificity and required big moves.

Let's make room in our minds to consider how many moves in our lives God initiated. By Providence through a call to pay taxes in one's hometown, God got Mary and Joseph to Bethlehem, and many other people in place. In the light of Providence, let's assess the depth of our submission and our willingness to trust God's guidance. There are many moving parts to destiny, and these parts are intertwined with the lives of many others.

Father, it is too easy to think about the direction of my life alone. I ask you to broaden my perspective as I seek to understand Providence. Open my eyes to the moves you designed in my life and cause me to see the impact of those moves. I pray this in Jesus' name. AMEN.

17

Finding God in the Good Place

In the sixth month the angel Gabriel was sent from God to a city of Galilee named Nazareth.

Luke 1:26 ESV

Sometimes, We Meet God in Certain Places.

I appreciate the detail in this verse. Elizabeth was not just pregnant; she was six months pregnant. An unnamed angel was kept back. God sent Gabriel. It is worth noting that Gabriel did not just poof! and appear, but God intentionally sent him. We could be okay with knowing that God sent Gabriel to the region called Galilee. But no, we learn that Gabriel was sent to a city called Nazareth.

How convinced are we that God sees us? This one verse proves that God knows where we are, and we can mark time by the progress others are making. He knows where we are and will send a messenger to our location. God has an intention; this is the significance of Nazareth.

We are never lost. We are always found. Selah.

Father, thank you for the significant places in my life where you have found me. And I found myself. Thank you in advance for each Nazareth in my future. In finding me, you remind me that you see me and know me better than anyone. For this and more, I am grateful. I pray this in Jesus' name. AMEN.

18

Finding God in the Restrictions

. . . for he will be great before the Lord. And he must not drink wine or strong drink, and he will be filled with the Holy Spirit, even from his mother's womb.

Luke 1:15 ESV

The Nazarite Vow is Recorded in Numbers 6:1-4.

The three parts of the Nazarite vow are restrictions, cleansing, and procedures for ending the vow. The word Nazarite means to abstain. Men and women could take the Nazarite vow for a set time frame or permanently. One under a Nazarite vow was seen as separated or consecrated to God.

Restrictions of the Nazarite vow included separation from strong wine and strong drink, no vinegar of any kind, and no grapes of any form – whole, juiced, or dried. Nazarites were not to have their hair cut until the vow ended. They also could not go near the dead.

Zechariah received an angelic visitation to announce parentage for him and Elizabeth. This baby would be a boy, great in God's eyes, forbidden from drinking wine and strong drink, and filled with the Holy Spirit in the womb.

Advent reminds us that we each have a role in God's unfolding story. There are expectations for each of us. As we learn contentment and submission, we find God in the restrictions or limits of consecration.

Father, thank you for the desire you put in me to know you and draw closer to you. As you lead me, help me to stay committed to your will for my life, especially in what you do not want me to do. I pray this in Jesus' name. AMEN.

19

Finding God in the Messenger

In the sixth month the angel Gabriel was sent from God to a city of Galilee named Nazareth.

Luke 1:26 ESV

Sometimes, We Find God in the Sent Ones.

The angel Gabriel is a reminder of God's attention to us, and God's ability to intervene in the schedule of our lives. Elizabeth rejoiced in being pregnant and left behind a disgraceful time of barrenness (Lk. 1:24-25). She was five months along. In her sixth month, God sent the arch angel Gabriel to Elizabeth's cousin, the virgin Mary.

We can read, journal, or hope silently in the heart. We can pray, fast, or make declarations of faith, in faith. What is expected is that we will live and greet one day after another. We will carry on routines and take care of errands. We will love, be loved, and show great care for others. What we will not do is rush God.

At a time of God's choosing, He will send one on a divine mission to us. Gabriel was sent to a virgin named Mary with an announcement. Our "Gabriel" may have a different task. The hope of Advent is that God sees us and will speak. Remember, he is here; and he is coming through his sent ones.

Father, thank you for knowing when we need special encouragement. You sent angels to calm fear and affirm your callings. Thank you in advance for the "Gabriel" people you will send. At the appointed time, allow my ear to hear and my heart to perceive your message. Let trust and obedience be my response. I pray this in Jesus' name. AMEN.

20

Finding God in the Questions

[18] And Zechariah said to the angel, "How shall I know this? For I am an old man, and my wife is advanced in years." [34] And Mary said to the angel, "How will this be, since I am a virgin?" [66] and all who heard them laid them up in their hearts, saying, "What then will this child be?" For the hand of the Lord was with him.

Luke 1:18, 34, 66 ESV

[1] Now after Jesus was born in Bethlehem of Judea in the days of Herod the king, behold, wise men from the east came to Jerusalem, [2] saying, "Where is he who has been born king of the Jews? For we saw his star when it rose and have come to worship him."

Matthew 2:1-2 ESV

Sometimes, We Find God When We Ask.

The Advent account has within it several questions. Zechariah asked for confirmation when the angel said that with Elizabeth, he would have a son (Lk. 1:18). At her angelic visitation, Mary asked how she could become pregnant as a virgin (v. 34). The people who witnessed Zechariah break the naming tradition to call his son John; they asked, "What then will this child become" (v. 66)? Finally, the wise men inquired on where to find the one born King of the Jews (Matt. 2:1-2).

Questions are one way we show interest. They are a sign that we want to know more. Like the examples mentioned above, we have different motives for asking. But we are all seeking. Advent is not a clean collection of stories with happy endings tied up in big and pretty bows. There are some holes, some missing details that inspire questions. How about we ask?

Let's not shy away from asking God about himself, the Scriptures, or the details of our lives. Whether for confirmation, curiosity, or guidance, let's ask to learn, discover, and grow.

Father, thank you for entertaining my questions and for answering. You are not intimidated when I do not understand and want to know more. Teach me to ask the right questions. Prepare me to receive your answers. I pray this in Jesus' name. AMEN.

21

Finding God in a Song

⁴⁶ And Mary said, "My soul magnifies the Lord, ⁴⁷ and my spirit rejoices in God my Savior, ⁴⁸ for he has looked on the humble estate of his servant. For behold, from now on all generations will call me blessed; ⁴⁹ for he who is mighty has done great things for me, and holy is his name. ⁵⁰ And his mercy is for those who fear him from generation to generation. ⁵¹ He has shown strength with his arm; he has scattered the proud in the thoughts of their hearts; ⁵² he has brought down the mighty from their thrones and exalted those of humble estate; ⁵³ he has filled the hungry with good things, and the rich he has sent away empty. ⁵⁴ He has helped his servant Israel, in remembrance of his mercy, ⁵⁵ as he spoke to our fathers, to Abraham and to his offspring forever."

Luke 1:46-55 ESV

Sometimes, We Just Need a Good Lyric to Express How We Feel.

We may send song lyrics or recordings to our loved ones because we cannot say what we feel any better than the song. Mary, the Mother of Jesus, had this experience. Her song is the Magnificat, and it is one of the treasures of Advent. The Magnificat is a song of praise honoring God's choice of Mary and the significance of the Christ child. Mary was a young lady chosen by God to carry and birth his physical expression on earth. We take this truth in stride today but try thinking through the marvel of immaculate conception.

Do we have miraculous testimonies that inspire us to sing in response to God's goodness? Advent reminds us that an inspired song honors God's will in us and his work in the world through our miracle.

Father, thank you for giving me a song. You are wonderful and I am grateful for your choosing me. Let my song always be to you. I pray this in Jesus' name. AMEN.

22

Finding God in the Support of Others

[41] And when Elizabeth heard the greeting of Mary, the baby leaped in her womb. And Elizabeth was filled with the Holy Spirit, [42] and she exclaimed with a loud cry, "Blessed are you among women, and blessed is the fruit of your womb!"

Luke 1:41-42 ESV

Sometimes, We Want Companions for Every Step When God Intends Special Moments on the Journey.

Advent reminds us that God builds support into our process. Mary carried the Son of God. Her cousin Elizabeth was pregnant with John the Baptist, the forerunner to the Son of God. Each experienced a miraculous conception, six months apart.

God will send someone who understands and celebrates the creative work of God in our lives. When Elizabeth heard Mary's greeting, Elizabeth's baby lept. Together Mary and Elizabeth rejoiced.

May the Advent remind us that God is greater than our feelings. We may feel unsupported or vulnerable in carrying out our divine tasks. We may wonder why others have crowds and what seems to us loads of support. Today though, let us elevate our minds and embrace our birthing partners – whoever they are, and however God sends them.

Father, whether stranger, family, or close friend, I accept support. Thank you for seeing me when I want or need to be seen. Thank you for the ways you show me you see me. I pray this in Jesus' name. AMEN.

23

Finding God in Spite of Giants

¹ In those days a decree went out from Caesar Augustus that all the world should be registered. ² This was the first registration when Quirinius was governor of Syria. ³ And all went to be registered, each to his own town.

Luke 2:1-3 ESV

Advent Reminds Us That Political Systems Are Under God's Watch.

He will use anything and anyone, unbeknownst to them, to serve his greater purpose. I like to compare the call to action in Luke 2:1-3 for Mary and Joseph to Esther's transition into the palace in the Book of Esther 2:1-8. God used powerful political men to issue decrees and edicts that required many people to move. In the move, Mary and Joseph, as well as Esther, were positioned for important experiences.

Emperor Augustus decreed that all of Rome should be counted and required citizens to be registered in their home-towns. Joseph took Mary to Bethlehem because he descended from David's lineage.

We know from Jesus' adult ministry that the Roman system – culture, policy, government, economy, etc. – was the backdrop for the introduction of the Kingdom of God. The perspective we gain is on God's sovereignty. While powerful men maneuver to build themselves and oppress others, God is in control.

Father, even Rome submits to your will. Thank you for being my sovereign God who has all things under your control. I pray this in Jesus' name. AMEN.

24

Finding God When He Finds Me

⁸ And in the same region there were shepherds out in the field, keeping watch over their flock by night. ⁹ And an angel of the Lord appeared to them, and the glory of the Lord shone around them, and they were filled with great fear. ¹⁰ And the angel said to them, "Fear not, for behold, I bring you good news of great joy that will be for all the people. ¹¹ For unto you is born this day in the city of David a Savior, who is Christ the Lord. ¹² And this will be a sign for you: you will find a baby wrapped in swaddling cloths and lying in a manger." ¹³ And suddenly there was with the angel a multitude of the heavenly host praising God

and saying,

¹⁴ "Glory to God in the highest, and on earth peace among those with whom he is pleased!" ¹⁵ When the angels went away from them into heaven, the shepherds said to one another, "Let us go over to Bethlehem and see this thing that has happened, which the Lord has made known to us." [16] And they went with haste and found Mary and Joseph, and the baby lying in a manger. [17] And when they saw it, they made known the saying that had been told them concerning this child. [18] And all who heard it wondered at what the shepherds told them. [19] But Mary treasured up all these things, pondering them in her heart. [20] And the shepherds returned, glorifying and praising God for all they had heard and seen, as it had been told them.

Luke 2:8-20 ESV

When God Needs to Get Word to Us, Our Location is Never a Barrier.

What a comfort! The shepherds are wonderful proof of God's ability to touch humanity with his message. Advent reminds us that even if we are spending the night at work in a field, he can still speak to us.

The shepherds received the Advent announcement first. An angel appeared before them, the glory of the Lord shining, and the praise of the heavenly host brought them the good news of great joy. They watched angels return to heaven and chose to find the Christ child.

More than receivers, the shepherds were givers. They told Mary and Joseph about their angelic encounter and what was said about the baby Jesus. The shepherds are not unlike us – focused on tasks at hand when divinely interrupted with important messages. Advent reminds us that the Lord knows where we are and can surprise us with revelation. Let us stay hopeful to receive and inspire to give.

Father, thank you for finding me and choosing me to share your message. Settle me in this truth that I may be content wherever I am and convinced that I am never outside of your reach. I pray this in Jesus' name. AMEN.

CHRISTMAS

25

Finding God When There Is No Pattern

¹⁵ He is the image of the invisible God, the firstborn of all creation. ¹⁶ For by him all things were created, in heaven and on earth, visible and invisible, whether thrones or dominions or rulers or authorities—all things were created through him and for him. ¹⁷ And he is before all things, and in him all things hold together.

Colossians 1:15-17 ESV

Without Question, Great is the Mystery of Godliness (1 Tim. 3:16).

In the letter to the church at Colossae, written many years after the ascension of Jesus, we learn that Jesus is the first born. Think about this. Years after the ascension of Jesus also means hundreds of years since the prophets, the kings, the tribes, and Adam and Eve. Yet Jesus is called the first born of all creation.

Colossians 1:15-17 is one way to explain why the Advent season is full of hope, because Christ is the sum of all things. He is Creator of all things; that includes us, beings made for him. Though physically born after years of other lives lived and prophecies given, Jesus is before all things. Sometimes, we must take a deep breath and love that God reserves the right to be mysterious.

The wonder and awe of Advent is wrapped up in the manifested Christ. Welcome, Jesus, to our world and into our hearts!

Father, thank you for the mystery of Advent. Fill my heart with wonder and awe at your greatness in my everyday life. I pray this in Jesus' name. AMEN.

EPIPHANY

26

Finding God in the Heavens

"Where is he who has been born king of the Jews? For we saw his star when it rose and have come to worship him."

Matthew 2:2 ESV

Epiphany Reminds Us That Even When Our Attention is Elsewhere, Jesus is the End of Our Search.

Jesus Christ is born, and there are 12 more days of Christmas to mark the journey of the magi and their arrival to the Christ child. Epiphany means manifestation, appearance, or appearing, and refers to the visual presence of a divine being.

The magi, who were also called wise men, were astrologers, priests, and royal advisors from Persia. As Gentiles, the magi asked in Jerusalem for the child born King of the Jews. They saw his star rising in the sky and went to worship him. Maybe unbeknownst to them, they were looking for Jesus.

Commentary in The Passion Translation (TPT) suggests the magi likely descended from the magi taught by the prophet Daniel (ch. 2). Daniel's prophecy of the Messiah's death may have allowed the magi to calculate Jesus' date of birth. This may be how the magi were able to see the star – be it comet, supernova, or conjunction of planets – and know the King of the Jews was born.

Father, thank you for redirecting me when I focus on other things. I pray this in Jesus' name. AMEN.

27

Finding God in a Dangerous Question

"Where is he who has been born king of the Jews? For we saw his star when it rose and have come to worship him."

Matthew 2:2 ESV

Sometimes, We Get Caught Up in the Drama Because of a Simple Question.

The magi, also called wise men, were Persian priests and astrologers. Once they knew the Christ was born, they travelled to see him. With one simple question, the wise men became part of a political plot.

The magi ignited a panic when they entered Jerusalem and asked where to find the King of the Jews. Herod, the king of Israel, was frightened at the prospect of competition and sought the opinions of experts. Chief priests and scribes recounted for Herod the words of the prophets. The Messiah would be born in Bethlehem and rule his people, Israel.

Epiphany reminds us that God opens our eyes when the time is right. Herod did not see competition in his future, much less a King of the Jews. Let us continue in hope for the Father to bring an epiphany to our loved ones and all lost souls.

Father, thank you for watching over me when my question is simple, and the circumstance is complex. Thank you for using a question to ignite a search for truth in other. If we all seek, may we all find you. I pray this in Jesus' name. AMEN.

28

Finding God in the Guiding Light

⁹ After listening to the king, they went on their way. And behold, the star that they had seen when it rose went before them until it came to rest over the place where the child was. ¹⁰ When they saw the star, they rejoiced exceedingly with great joy.

Matthew 2:9-10 ESV

Everyone Needs Some Direction Now and Again.

The star is a major player in the Advent and Epiphany accounts. As the guiding light to the location of the Christ child, the star reminds us that God gives signals within our frames of reference. The wise men were astrologers; they studied the position of the stars relative to earthly events.

To those who studied the stars God led by a star! This is a marvelous Epiphany reminder of God's ability to lead us, and his desire for us to understand his messages. For the wise men, the star offered directions to reach the Christ child. For us, the star may be photos for the photographer, a stethoscope for the nurse or doctor, a script for the actor or playwright, and so on.

Sometimes, we find God on the way, and we must follow his light. We may have but a few details, and he fills in the gaps in our knowledge. He leads us like he led the wise men by the star.

Father, thank you for guiding my life. Help me to recognize every signal you send and respond properly. When I miss the cue, thank you for setting me back on a good course. I pray this in Jesus' name. AMEN.

29

Finding God with a Heart of Honor

"Where is he who has been born king of the Jews? For we saw his star when it rose and have come to worship him."

Matthew 2:2 ESV

Epiphany is a Reminder That Honor is a Timeless Motive.

The magi expressed their motive for finding the newborn King of the Jews. Worship. Homage. Honor. This is a powerful point for meditation for several reasons.

1. The magi made a 12-day journey to show honor.

2. The gifts of the magi were expressions of worship.

3. The hearts of the magi were postured to give. The return was getting to see the Christ child.

4. The honor was for the King in the baby.

Let us embrace the heart of the magi to worship and pay homage to the King. We can bring him our gifts and our lives. We can rejoice to be in his presence.

Father, I want to live a life that honors you. Please help me to make honoring you the priority of my heart and mind. I pray this in Jesus' name. AMEN.

30

Finding God in Humanity

[34] And Mary said to the angel, "How will this be, since I am a virgin?" [35] And the angel answered her, "The Holy Spirit will come upon you, and the power of the Most High will overshadow you; therefore the child to be born will be called holy—the Son of God."

Luke 1:34-35 ESV

How Easy is it for Us to Wrap Our Minds Around God Being Born?

Be honest. Jesus has a physical birthday (accuracy on when we celebrate is both informative and moot). Jesus has a place in the family order. God is a baby, as well as Creator, Savior, Atonement, and Resurrection. Wow.

Advent makes faith simple. Advent also challenges how we see God. Lion, Lamb, Savior, Friend, Lord… and, baby? How do we see God? Today, I want us to see all his goodness inside an infant. There's a sweet awareness to see our Great God helpless, harmless, and swaddled, while also the consolation of Israel.

God being born in flesh is the greatest display of emotional intelligence. In Advent, God arrives the way of all flesh. There is a point of identification that causes us to marvel, and him to be merciful. For God to connect with us in this way encourages our hope and faith.

Father, thank you for choosing to walk in my footsteps as a human. Thank you for bringing divinity to me in more relatable ways than I can count. I am grateful you were born. I pray this in Jesus' name. AMEN.

31

Finding God in His Divinity

And going into the house, they saw the child with Mary his mother, and they fell down and worshiped him. Then, opening their treasures, they offered him gifts, gold and frankincense and myrrh.

Matthew 2:11 ESV

Epiphany Reminds Us That God Himself Can Be Found.

The magi brought three gifts to the baby Jesus – gold, frank-incense, and myrrh. Gold represents the deity of Christ. The baby is God. This is one of the great marvels of the Advent, that God reduced himself first to humanity, and then to be naturally born as an infant.

How far will people go to identify with us, to put them-selves in our shoes? Some will not go far at all. But God chose us so fiercely that he contained divinity in his human body. Wow, God created a new dimension for leveling up!

When we find God, we can offer him our lives. We are the gold, you know. The proof of God's divinity is a surrendered vessel indwelt by his Holy Spirit.

Father, thank you for taking on a body to walk in my shoes. I bring you the gold of my life – all that you have invested in me. Help me to nurture and grow it, and bring you glory. I pray this in Jesus' name. AMEN.

32

Finding God in Service

And going into the house, they saw the child with Mary his mother, and they fell down and worshiped him. Then, opening their treasures, they offered him gifts, gold and frankincense and myrrh.

Matthew 2:11 ESV

Epiphany Reminds Us That Jesus Would Grow to Live a Life of Service.

The wise men brought a gift of frankincense to the baby Jesus. Frankincense is a sweet-smelling incense and represents Christ's life of holiness, excellence, and devotion. To a baby, the wise men brought an honor offering for the life the baby would live.

Advent and Epiphany have many entrance points to reach different kinds of people. One way is service. We can meet God as we serve him. We allow the finished work of Jesus to work in us, make us holy, and commit to serving him through serving others. In three years of public ministry, Jesus touched and is touching the world. Let us resolve to serve with impact and be mindful of the reach of our Savior.

Father, thank you for your service. Your example is teaching me the power of service. Be glorified in my service to the Kingdom. Allow me to touch lives that will serve you. I pray this in Jesus' name. AMEN.

33

Finding God in Sacrifice

*And going into the house, they saw the child with Mary
his mother, and they fell down and worshiped him. Then,
opening their treasures, they offered him gifts, gold and
frankincense and myrrh.*

Matthew 2:11 ESV

In Every Death There is a Life.

The third gift of the magi to the Christ child was myrrh, an embalming spice. The myrrh gift acknowledged what Jesus would grow and endure in death on the stake. Epiphany reminds us that sacrifice is built in to the greatest of loves.

Through the myrrh, Epiphany is a reminder of two things. We have one life, first of all; and God's attached to it a divine purpose. Secondly, life is never free of sacrifice; and, I will add, tradeoffs. We will have to put the proverbial "it" on the line in exchange for our purpose. Myrrh reminds us that there is an arc to Jesus' life that includes his death as a sacrifice. May we learn to number our days, value our time, and be grateful for God's breath in our bodies.

Father, thank you for my life. Thank you for your redemptive work, beginning with your birth. I am alive because you chose your Kingdom task over everything else. Grant me a sober view of sacrifice so that I will not fear any part of my service to you. I pray this in Jesus' name. AMEN.

34

Finding God in the Anomalies

*"Where is he who has been born king of the Jews? For we
saw his star when it rose and have come to worship him."*

Matthew 2:2 ESV

Epiphany Reinforces Our Faith in God's Ability to do the Impossible.

We must admit the oddity of a promised Messiah fulfilled in a baby. Did the true believers of that time imagine their Messiah as an infant? Epiphany is one of the ways God operates in what RT Kendall calls "extreme variations." A baby who is a king? What boggles the natural mind makes perfect spiritual sense! Let us boldly hold to our conviction. If God can put his kingship in a baby, then what can he make of us?

Father, give me to see you in the different and odd things. Thank you for the potential in the anomalies. May the treasure you placed in my earthen vessel be unlocked and bravely used to bring you glory. I pray this in Jesus' name. AMEN.

35

Finding God in the Evidence

After listening to the king, they went on their way. And behold, the star that they had seen when it rose went before them until it came to rest over the place where the child was.

Matthew 2:9 ESV

For the Wise Men, the Stars Did Not Lie.

At Herod's orders, the magi set off to find the Christ child. They followed the star until it stopped over Jesus' location. They entered the house and found Mary and baby Jesus. Epiphany reminds us that faith becomes sight. Years of prophetic words and pictures will manifest. The abstract will become concrete, and we will experience with our natural senses what we hold to in our imaginations by faith. There will be proof of our belief.

Father, thank you for faith made sight. I will see what I believe. Help my unbelief. I pray this in Jesus' name. AMEN.

36

Finding God in Protection

And being warned in a dream not to return to Herod, they departed to their own country by another way.

Matthew 2:12 ESV

Epiphany Reminds Us That Innocence Deserves Protection.

Herod commissioned the magi to go to Bethlehem on a mission to find the Christ child. Once they found Mary and Jesus, they paid homage. When the magi offered their gifts to the baby Jesus, their mission was complete. Herod asked for the magi to return with the location of the child.

But God warned the magi in a dream: do not return to Herod. Herod claimed a desire to worship, but it was a false claim. This divine interruption allowed the magi to head back to their own country on a road that would avoid Herod.

God desires to protect us like he protected Jesus from being found by Herod. Sometimes the magi in our lives do not recognize or pay attention to God speaking. Sadly, some of us must suffer as a result. Epiphany can renew our hope in God's good plan and intention for us.

Father, thank you for giving me warnings. Open my eyes to see the signs and follow your wisdom. I pray this in Jesus' name. AMEN.

37

Finding God on the Way

² Now after Jesus was born in Bethlehem of Judea in the days of Herod the king, behold, wise men from the east came to Jerusalem, . . . ¹² And being warned in a dream not to return to Herod, they departed to their own country by another way . . .

14-15a And he rose and took the child and his mother by night and departed to Egypt and remained there until the death of Herod . . . 21 And he rose and took the child and his mother and went to the land of Israel . . . 23 And he went and lived in a city called Nazareth . . .

Matthew 2:1, 12, 14-15a, 21, 23a ESV

Sometimes, the Important Things Happen on the Journey.

Everyone involved in the Advent and Epiphany accounts took a journey. Whether from one place to another, or from one state of mind or faith to another, God's plan required a move. There are some things that are common to us all in the walk of faith. Journeys are one of those common things. We each must confront a new place or perspective to move ahead in God's will and plan.

Epiphany reminds us that process is permanent for the faith walk. God will challenge us to make requisite moves to a new place or a new perspective to complete his task. Or he may ask us to do a thing or believe in him for a supernatural result. We can find him on the way.

Father, thank you for every journey. Help me when my focus shifts to the minor things so that I can receive from the journey all that I am to receive. I want to learn every lesson. I pray this in Jesus' name. AMEN.

BONUS

38

Finding God Everywhere

And blessed is she who believed that there would be a fulfillment of what was spoken to her from the Lord."

Luke 1:45 ESV

Anything Can Happen.

I cannot explain my fixation with Advent. My upbringing emphasized the Christmas story – baby Jesus, wise men, angels, Mary, Joseph, speeches and plays performed at church, songs and carols, and gifts. I grew up appreciating the reason for the season and loved what the holiday season did for people. Humanity seemed nicer and more aware of one another during the holidays.

Along the way, I discovered Advent. I liked that there seemed to be more ceremony around the Christ and the season, as well as other players in the nativity. Everyone had a place, and my scope increased; I am part of the story of the Christ. Like the miracles of Jesus, the interactions, and the resurrection, I also have a role in his advent. It was powerful insight for me. The more I studied, my scope kept increasing. Advent is wild card season.

In decks of cards there are jokers. In the popular Uno card game, there are wild cards. Wild cards allow the player to move with freedom. To me, Advent is God's wild card. A jealous and wayward king, astrologers, shepherds, an emperor, a census, long journeys, short trips in the region, animals, gold and spices, angels, dreams, miracle pregnancies, and more! Advent is a time where tired hope gets a big hug from God and believing is possible again.

Father, thank you for the advent season and every reminder that you can move the world to get me in the right place to fulfill your promise in my life. Thank you for divine visitations and messengers to help me move from fear to faith in walking with you. I pray this in Jesus' name. AMEN.

39

Finding God in the Present

*For unto you is born this day in the city of David a Savior,
who is Christ the Lord.*

Luke 2:11 ESV

Marking the Advent Every Year is a Reminder of the Prescence of God.

There are times when I wonder if God is with me or listening to my prayers. I know in my head that he is always with me and promised to never leave me or abandon me. But my feelings say other things sometimes, and I wonder where he is in a situation, or why I do not have the answer I need yet.

Advent is the multifaceted account of the birth of God as Jesus. We can focus on the origins of the Christmas holidays, or the feelgood stories of a jolly man who brings presents to children everywhere. Or we can focus on what the presence of God in the earth means to humanity. He is here – meaning, he is born and present on earth. He is coming – meaning, Jesus is still available to make entrances in our lives. Whether by saving faith, visitation, encouragement, or warning and instruction, the entrance of Jesus is as important now as it was the first time.

I hope that these meditation thoughts help us reframe our approach to daily living as well as the holiday season. Jesus is not a myth. Jesus is God, and he is real. Jesus is the flesh of God born to show us a perfect human example through the power of divinity. He is here! And he is coming – as we welcome him into our lives, homes, vocations, and service, he will join us and lead us into obedience and godly harvest.

Father, thank you for understanding better than anyone what it is like to be human. Thank you for taking on a body to experience life and all its parts. I invite you into my life, my home, my decisions, and all I attempt to do and be. I pray this in Jesus' name. AMEN.

40

Finding God in High Praise

[13] And suddenly there was with the angel a multitude of the heavenly host praising God, and saying, [14] "Glory to God in the highest, and on earth peace, goodwill toward men!"

Luke 2:13-14 KJV

How Do You Respond When God Does Something Great?

To each his own, I am sure. There are many ways we are exhorted to respond to God's great works: praise, worship, obedience, service, loving others, increased commitment, and more. But how do we respond to God's greatest act of allowing himself to be limited by a body for the human experience? I do not know that we can respond, other than with the availability of our lives.

After the angel appeared to the shepherds with the announcement of the birth of the Christ, a multitude of the heavenly host joined in to praise God. The angels proclaimed glory to God, peace, and goodwill, or a good hope. This is the spirit of Advent, that the presence of Jesus Christ would bring peace and goodwill to humanity. Add this to the knowledge of God's love for us and others, acceptance of grace and spiritual gifts, and awareness of our areas of service, and what an influential force would be the body of Christ!

Glory to God in the highest! On earth, and where I live, let there be peace and goodwill towards men. Father, ignite and re-ignite our hope in you. Make me an instrument of your peace. I pray this in Jesus' name. AMEN.

About the Author

Shaunta D. Scroggins is an adult educator and public speaker for sacred and secular audiences. She is the founder and curator of The Bereans' Commentary, a growing online collection of personal and feature guest commentary on the Holy Bible. For more than 20 years, she has focused on the relevant design of knowledge exchanges and educational experiences for adults, be they classes, trainings, workshops, or open forums. Her mission is to help adult learners understand their significance and unique contribution through leader and Christian education. She is also the author of Altar Working. This is her second book.

For booking, please send inquiries to info@mybereanlife. com.

CPSIA information can be obtained
at www.ICGtesting.com
Printed in the USA
LVHW080249190122
708893LV00013B/531

9 781737 926214